Success With

Reading Comprehension

D1566781

■ SCHOLASTIC

Editor: Ourania Papacharalambous
Cover design by Tannaz Fassihi; cover illustration by Kevin Zimmer
Interior design by Cynthia Ng
Interior illustrations by Doug Jones (spot art); Mike Moran (6, 8, 12, 14, 18, 20–22, 24, 26, 28–34, 36, 40, 42, 44, 46)
All other images © Shutterstock.com

ISBN 978-1-338-79863-0
Scholastic Inc., 557 Broadway, New York, NY 10012
Copyright © 2022 Scholastic Inc.
All rights reserved. Printed in the U.S.A.
First printing, January 2022
1 2 3 4 5 6 7 8 9 10   40   29 28 27 26 25 24 23 22

INTRODUCTION

Reading can be fun when high-interest stories are paired with puzzles, interesting facts, and engaging activities. Parents and teachers alike will find *Scholastic Success With Reading Comprehension* to be a valuable educational tool. It is designed to help students in the fifth grade improve their reading comprehension skills. Students will practice finding the main idea and story details, making inferences, following directions, drawing conclusions, and sequencing. They are also challenged to develop vocabulary, understand cause and effect, distinguish between fact and opinion. On page 4, you will find a list of the key skills covered in the activities throughout this book. Practicing and reviewing these important reading skills will help students become better readers. Remember to praise them for their efforts and successes!

TABLE OF CONTENTS

Grade-Appropriate Skills Covered in *Scholastic Success With Reading Comprehension: Grade 5*

Quote accurately from a text when explaining what the text says explicitly and when drawing inferences from the text.

Determine a theme of a story, drama, or poem from details in the text, including how characters in a story or drama respond to challenges or how the speaker in a poem reflects upon a topic; summarize the text.

Compare and contrast two or more characters, settings, or events in a story or drama, drawing on specific details in the text.

Determine the meaning of words and phrases as they are used in a text, including figurative language such as metaphors and similes.

Compare and contrast stories in the same genre on their approaches to similar themes and topics.

Determine two or more main ideas of a text and explain how they are supported by key details; summarize the text.

Determine the meaning of general academic and domain-specific words and phrases in a text relevant to a grade 5 topic or subject area.

Know and apply grade-level phonics and word analysis skills in decoding words.

Read with sufficient accuracy and fluency to support comprehension.

Write informative/explanatory texts to examine a topic and convey ideas and information clearly.

Write narratives to develop real or imagined experiences or events using effective technique, descriptive details, and clear event sequences.

Demonstrate command of the conventions of standard English grammar and usage when writing or speaking.

Demonstrate command of the conventions of standard English capitalization, punctuation, and spelling when writing.

Use knowledge of language and its conventions when writing, speaking, reading, or listening.

Determine or clarify the meaning of unknown and multiple-meaning words and phrases based on grade 5 reading and content, choosing flexibly from a range of strategies.

Demonstrate understanding of figurative language, word relationships, and nuances in word meanings.

A Terrific Trip!

Read the letter Kelly received from her friend this summer. Then, answer the questions about the letter.

The **main idea** tells what a story or paragraph is mostly about.

Dear Kelly,

We are having a great time in Washington, D.C. Today, we visited two monuments.

I am sure you have seen pictures of the famous Washington Monument. It is a huge obelisk, over 55 feet in height and covered in white marble. The monument weighs over 90,000 tons! We took an elevator to the top of the monument and had a great view of the whole city. In the lobby, at the base of the obelisk, is a statue of our first president, George Washington. This spectacular monument honors him.

Next, we visited a very different monument, the Vietnam Veterans Memorial. This monument is two walls of polished black granite arranged in a V-shape. On the walls are carved the names of more than 58,000 men and women who gave their lives in service in the Vietnam War. Visitors walk very quietly and respectfully along the granite walls. All along the base of the monument are flowers, flags, and small memorials left by friends and family members. There is so much more we have to see here in Washington, D.C. I'll tell you all about our trip when I get home.

See you soon,
Megan

1 What is the main idea of Paragraph 2?

○ The Washington Monument honors our nation's first president.
○ The Washington Monument must have taken a long time to build.
○ The Washington Monument is a massive, impressive structure.

2 What is the main idea of Paragraph 3?

○ Visitors to the Vietnam Veterans Memorial often leave gifts along the granite walls.
○ A visit to the Vietnam Veterans Memorial is a very moving experience.
○ The Vietnam Memorial consists of two granite walls arranged in a V-shape.

The Louisiana Purchase

When Thomas Jefferson became president of the United States in 1801, the Louisiana Territory and the Floridas were part of Spain. The two countries had treaties that allowed American farmers and merchants to use the shipping ports in these areas. But, in 1802, Spain revoked American access to the warehouses in the port of New Orleans and turned over control of the Louisiana Territory to France. Not only was Jefferson furious, he was also scared.

The French dictator, Napoleon Bonaparte, had a huge military force and hopes of expanding the French Empire. With France now controlling the Louisiana Territory, Jefferson feared that Napoleon wanted to expand into North America and even the United States. Jefferson sent diplomats to France and instructed them to find a solution.

While Jefferson's diplomats made their way to France, an ongoing rebellion of enslaved persons and free Blacks in the French colony of Saint-Domingue (present-day Haiti) intensified. This long-simmering conflict soon spiraled into a full-fledged revolution. Struggling with the loss of income from Haitian plantations, an outbreak of yellow fever among French troops fighting there, and a looming war with England, France decided to sell the Louisiana Territory.

On April 30, 1803, a "Treaty of Purchase between the United States and the French Republic" was made between the two countries. Although it has long been maintained that the United States acquired nearly 600 million acres of land for $15 million, the United States actually purchased only the right to acquire these lands from Native American peoples who had lived on these lands long before Europeans came to North America.

The Purchase provided enormous incentive to continue expanding the United States, encouraging further westward migration and intensifying the displacement of Native peoples.

Although the United States and its private citizens paid some Native American nations small amounts for their land,

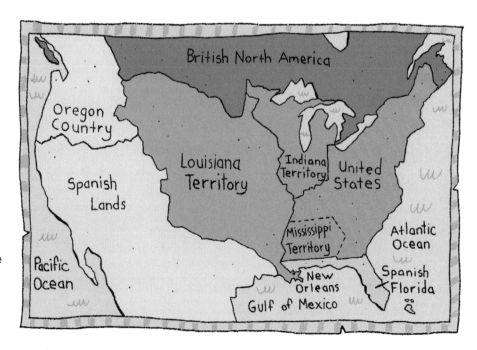

other Native American nations received no money, being made victims to unfair treaties and discriminatory policies. By 1840, the U.S. had forced tens of thousands of Native Americans from their lands along what became known as the Trail of Tears. More than 5,000 people died during the forced migration.

Acquiring the Louisiana Territory almost doubled the area of the United States, greatly increased the size and role of the federal government, and marked a future where the government would actively seek to expand its holdings and promote private economic activity. While the Purchase created all or parts of 15 states, including Louisiana, Arkansas, Missouri, Iowa, North Dakota, South Dakota, Nebraska, Kansas, Wyoming, Minnesota, Oklahoma, Colorado, and Montana, the Purchase's negative impact on Native American peoples, the physical environment, and the relationship between Americans and Native Americans is incalculable.

1 What is the main idea of Paragraph 2?

○ The United States was threatened by French control of the Louisiana Territory.
○ Spain owned two major territories in North America.
○ Thomas Jefferson wanted to purchase only New Orleans.

2 What is the main idea of Paragraph 6?

○ Thomas Jefferson was proud of the accomplishments of his presidency.
○ The United States doubled its size with the purchase of the Louisiana Territory.
○ While acquiring the Louisiana Territory greatly transformed the United States, Native American peoples were negatively impacted by the purchase.

3 How do you think the United States would be different if France had not agreed to sell the Louisiana Territory?

_____

_____

_____

_____

_____

_____

A REAL Princess

Jason and Theo worked all day on their writing assignment. They had to choose a fairy tale and rewrite it. The fairy tale had to be written as if it were a story that could appear in a magazine today. They decided to use a fairy tale by Hans Christian Andersen. They had learned that Andersen was born in Denmark in 1805. His fairy tales have delighted young children all over the world for many years. Jason and Sam were very pleased with their modern version of the classic fairy tale *The Princess and the Pea*.

Details in a story provide the reader with information about the main idea and help the reader better understand the story.

A Happy Ending

As some of you may have heard, the Queen has finally ended her search for a real princess to marry the Prince. She had been looking for a very long time. In her quest, the Queen had certain requirements that she knew only a real princess could fulfill. For example, the Queen knew that only a real princess could . . . play the piano and harp at the same time, eat an ice cream cone without ever having the ice cream drip, read three months' worth of books in an afternoon, and feel a pea placed under a mattress.

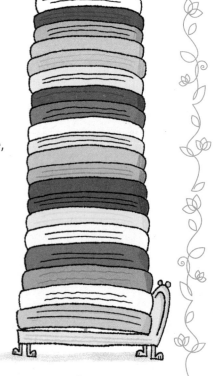

Even after searching all over the world, the Queen and the Prince could not find a real princess. They returned home very saddened. However, all hope was not lost! During the terrible storm last Tuesday night, a rain-soaked young woman showed up at the palace, asking for shelter. She claimed she was a princess. The Queen decided to test her. She hid a pea under 20 mattresses and 20 feather beds. To her delight, the girl slept terribly, for only a real princess can feel a pea beneath all those mattresses and feather beds.

So, under the most joyous of circumstances, the whole kingdom is invited to the royal wedding of the Prince and his real princess this Saturday at 4:00 P.M. at the palace.

Use the story to answer the questions.

1 What was the Queen looking for? _____

_____

2 Why was the Queen saddened after her search? _____

_____

_____

3 When did the real princess arrive at the palace? Be specific. _____

_____

_____

4 How did the Queen try to determine if the young woman was a real princess?

_____

_____

5 Do you think the Queen or the Prince was more concerned about finding a real

princess? Why? _____

_____

_____

6 How do you think the authors of the article feel about the wedding? _____

_____

7 When and where was Hans Christian Andersen born? _____

_____

8 Why did Jason and Sam change the original version of "The Princess and the Pea"?

_____

_____

Amazing Animals

All animals are fascinating, and some are truly amazing! For example, did you know that sharks' teeth are almost as hard as steel, or that kangaroo rats can survive longer without water than camels? Did you know that most of the animals on our planet don't have backbones? They are called **invertebrates** and make up about 97 percent of animals. Animals that do have backbones are **vertebrates**. Study the chart below to learn more about several amazing animals.

Animal	Where It Lives	Vertebrate or Invertebrate	Fascinating Fact
albatross	near most oceans	vertebrate	can sleep while flying
caterpillar	all over the world	invertebrate	has about four times as many muscles as humans
chameleon	forests in Africa and Madagascar	vertebrate	can move its eyes in two different directions at the same time
crocodile	tropical climates	vertebrate	eats only about 50 meals a year
giant squid	oceans throughout the world	invertebrate	has eyes bigger than a baby's head
giraffe	grasslands in Africa	vertebrate	tallest land animal; has only seven neck bones
octopus	oceans throughout the world	invertebrate	has three hearts
penguin	in the southern half of the world with cold ocean waters	vertebrate	eggs kept warm by male until hatched
shark	oceans throughout the world	vertebrate	never runs out of teeth
snail	almost everywhere— forests, deserts, rivers, ponds, oceans	invertebrate	can sleep for almost three years without waking up
sperm whale	oceans throughout the world	vertebrate	can hold its breath for up to 90 minutes

Use the chart to answer the questions.

1 Which animals live in the ocean?

_____

_____

_____

_____

2 What do the giant squid and the chameleon have in common?

_____

_____

_____

3 What vertebrates live in the ocean?

_____

_____

4 Which animals live all, or nearly all, over the world?

_____

_____

_____

_____

_____

5 Which animal can sleep while flying?

_____

6 Which animal eats an average of about once a week?

_____

7 What is fascinating about a chameleon's eyes?

_____

_____

_____

8 Which animal is a "super snoozer"?

_____

9 Which animal can hold its breath for over an hour?

_____

10 Which animal has only seven bones in its neck?

_____

Let's Eat Out

Context clues are words or sentences that can help a reader determine the meaning of a new word.

Reese was **famished**! It was nearly two o'clock, and he had not eaten since breakfast. Reese asked his mom if they could stop for lunch on their way home from his baseball game. They never ate out, but she agreed to **indulge** him to lunch at a restaurant. He had worked so hard keeping his grades up while on the baseball team.

She had always been careful to eat healthy foods. She explained to Reese that although eating out was **convenient** and often very tasty, it was usually not as healthy as eating home cooked meals. He **definitely** liked eating out, but he knew that the **nutritious** foods his mother made at home were good for him.

While waiting for their meal, Reese's mother began to talk about some of the **distinctive** foods eaten by people around the world. In China, for example, some restaurants serve bird's nest soup made from the nests of swallows. Reese was not aware that in Colombia moviegoers may purchase paper cones filled with roasted ants as a snack. His mother also told him about fugu, a special kind of fish served in Japanese restaurants. If not prepared correctly, fugu can be highly **toxic**. Those who cook it must be specially trained, so that diners do not get sick or die from their meal.

Looking at Reese's face, his mother took **pity** on him and promised to stop talking about food. Their food hadn't arrived yet, and all this talk about different kinds of food made Reese hungry.

Finally, the food arrived. Reese happily ate his lunch. Now all he wanted was an ice cream cone for dessert.

1 Write one of the bold words from the story for each definition below.
Use context clues to help.

a. to give in to the wishes of _____

b. sympathy _____

c. easy to reach _____

d. starving _____

e. certainly _____

f. healthy _____

g. poisonous _____

h. different _____

2 What does it mean to say a meal is nutritious? _____

_____

_____

3 What are three nutritious foods that you enjoy? _____

_____

_____

4 What distinctive foods have you heard about that you would like to try? Describe one.

_____

_____

_____

 Do some research about vitamins. On another sheet of paper, list eight words from the information you read that are unfamiliar to you. Use context clues to write a definition for each word. Then, look up each word in a dictionary to see if you are correct.

Terrific Territories

A United States territory is a **region** that belongs to the United States but is not one of the 50 states. A territory is under the control of the U.S. government, but it does not have representation in the national government. Despite their lack of representation in the national government, all territories govern themselves to a **limited extent**.

Territorial government is an old **institution**. The first American territory, the Northwest Territory, was set up in 1787. Until 1867, all territories were created in mainland areas of the United States. Then, in 1867, the United States purchased Alaska, and the first territory not directly connected with the rest of the states was **established**. **Gradually**, the United States **acquired** other **distant** lands.

In the past, territories often became states. Alaska and Hawaii were the last two territories that were admitted as states. Currently, the United States has control of over 10 territories. They include Puerto Rico, Guam, the U.S. Virgin Islands, American Samoa, Midway Islands, Wake Island, Johnston Atoll, Baker Island, Howland Island, Jarvis Island, Kingman Reef, Navassa Island, and Palmyra Atoll.

Since 1901, the Supreme Court and Congress have classified most territories as either incorporated or unincorporated. Incorporated territories are **entitled** to all rights **guaranteed** by the Constitution. The last two incorporated territories were Alaska and Hawaii. Unincorporated territories are guaranteed only **fundamental** rights.

1 Circle the correct definition for each bold word below.
Use context clues from the story to help.

a.	**limited extent**	excessive	partly	abundant
b.	**institution**	church	insulating device	established practice
c.	**gradually**	frequently	currently	over time
d.	**acquired**	sold	ascertained	bought
e.	**entitled**	has the right to	has the desire for	entrusted
f.	**guaranteed**	protected	licensed	promised
g.	**fundamental**	basic	inalienable	proper
h.	**distant**	further	faraway	foreign
i.	**region**	state	area	country
j.	**established**	finished	separated	created

2 Label *I* for incorporated and *U* for unincorporated

_____ a territory that is guaranteed all rights by the Constitution

_____ a territory that is guaranteed only basic rights

3 Which territory, purchased by the United States, was the first territory not to be

directly connected to the rest of the states? _____

4 Which were the last two territories to become states? _____

_____

5 Name three territories that the United States currently controls. _____

_____

 Do some research about one of the United States territories. On another
sheet of paper, list five new words you learned from the article. Then, write
a definition for each word.

Magnificent Musicians

To **compare** and **contrast** ideas in a passage, a reader determines how the ideas are alike and how they are different.

Kyle and Cassidy had to write a report together on a famous musician. They had one problem—they could not decide which musician to choose. Kyle wanted to do the report on John Philip Sousa (1854–1932), an American composer and bandmaster. Cassidy wanted to do it on Ludwig van Beethoven (1770–1827), a German composer.

Kyle was impressed by Beethoven's talent. But he favored Sousa because of his ability to write such a wide variety of music. Sousa wrote operettas, songs, waltzes, and his famous marches. Sousa took simple military marches and perked them up with a new and exciting rhythm. Kyle's favorites were *Semper Fidelis* and *The Stars and Stripes Forever*.

Cassidy also liked Sousa's marches and had even performed some dance routines to a couple of them. However, she was impressed with the variety of musical works Beethoven created. She loved to play his symphonies, sonatas, and concertos on the piano. She especially enjoyed the classical and romantic pieces Beethoven composed, like *Moonlight Sonata* and the opera *Fidelio*.

Kyle would not have minded focusing on Beethoven because he found him fascinating. He knew that Beethoven began losing his hearing when he was in his twenties and eventually became deaf during the last years of his life. Kyle was intrigued that, through all his hearing loss, Beethoven continued composing until he died at age 56. Still, Kyle preferred to study an American-born composer.

Cassidy felt it did not matter where the composer was born. She admired Beethoven's optimism and faith in moral values, which, she said, came through in his music. She believed that Beethoven helped composers gain the freedom to express themselves. Before his time, composers usually wrote music to teach, to entertain people at social functions, or for religious purposes. Thanks to Beethoven, music became something to enjoy for its own sake.

Cassidy did, however, admire the fact that Sousa made the United States Marine Band one of the finest in the world. He was appointed leader of this band in 1880. Cassidy's father, who was a career marine, said that it was because of this fantastic band that he wanted Cassidy to play an instrument.

So, how were Kyle and Cassidy to decide on whom to write their report? Both musicians were incredibly talented and had a great influence on the world of music. Finally, Cassidy suggested they flip a coin. Heads they would choose Sousa, tails they would choose Beethoven. Kyle tossed the coin high in the air . . .

1 Use the Venn diagram below to compare and contrast Beethoven and Sousa.

operettas	German	deaf	marches	composer
American	1770–1827	*Semper Fidelis*	influenced music	*Moonlight Sonata*
1854–1932	piano	respected worldwide	United States Marine Band	opera

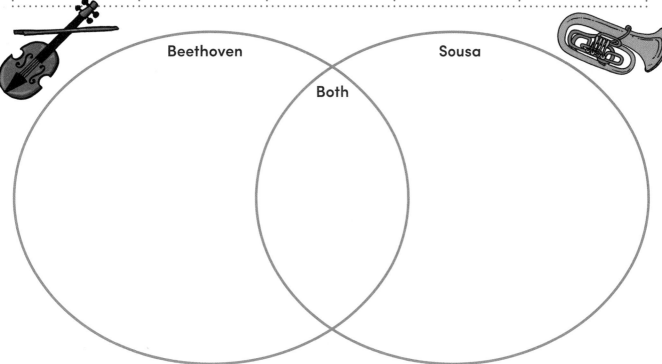

Beethoven   Sousa

Both

2 List two reasons each student preferred a particular musician.

Cassidy _____   Kyle _____

_____   _____

_____   _____

_____   _____

_____   _____

Read about two other musicians. On another sheet of paper, write three similarities and three differences about them.

Cinderellas Around the World

When Ms. Price told her students they were going to read *Cinderella*, they all groaned, saying they already knew that story. Ms. Price said that they certainly knew one version of *Cinderella*. She explained that *Cinderella* was a folk tale with many different versions found all over the world. She asked the students to research these different versions of *Cinderella*. They were going to have to give a summary about the *Cinderella* story they found. When the students returned to class, they were excited by all the different versions they found.

Kara told a *Cinderella* story from Ireland. A young lady named Trembling has two wicked sisters. The sisters leave Trembling to do all the housework while they go to church. Soon, a woman appears. She magically makes beautiful gowns for Trembling as a reward for her kindness. Each Sunday, Trembling stands outside the church door wearing a beautiful gown, and everyone admires her beauty. When people try to talk to her, she rides quickly away on a beautiful horse. One Sunday, a prince gets hold of her blue shoe as she rides off. Determined to marry the person whose foot fits the shoe, the prince travels through the village until he finds her. However, before the prince can marry her, he must fight all the other men in the village who also want to marry her. The prince wins and marries Trembling.

Marcos shared a *Cinderella* story from India. In this version a young lady's mother is magically transformed into a goat. A few years later her father remarries. The new stepmother is very cruel to her stepchildren, making them work hard and giving them little food. When the stepmother finds out that the family goat is magically providing her stepchildren with food, she has the goat killed. Even though the goat bones are buried in the ground, the stepchildren are still able to magically get food whenever they ask for it. One day when the stepdaughter is washing her face in the river, her nose ring falls into the water. It is eaten by a fish, which is later caught and prepared as a dinner for the king. When the king hears that a nose ring had been found in his fish, he sends word throughout the kingdom that the owner of the ring should come to the palace. The king meets the stepdaughter and marries her because of her beauty and kindness.

After sharing these stories, the students were surprised to find out that Cinderella was such a popular story, told in so many different ways and in so many countries around the world.

1 Complete the chart below about the two Cinderella versions.
Parts of it have been completed for you.

Country	cruel family members	main character is beautiful and kind	magic helper	object that proves identity	happy ending
Ireland		yes			marries prince
India			goat		

2 What happens in the Cinderella story you knew before reading these versions?
Complete the following chart based on the story you know.

Your version of Cinderella	cruel family members	main character is beautiful and kind	magic helper	object that proves identity	happy ending

3 What characteristics do the two versions of Cinderella seem to have in common?

_____

_____

4 Where are the biggest differences in the versions? _____

_____

_____

5 Why do you think there are so many similar stories around the world?

_____

_____

 Research more Cinderella stories from other parts of the world. Then, on another sheet of paper, write your own version of Cinderella. Be sure to include all the necessary characteristics, but feel free to make changes in the time, setting, and to some of the characters. Read your story to a friend.

No Baking Required

To **sequence** is to put the events of a story in the order in which they happen.

Max was disappointed. He came home from school excited to eat his dad's famous chocolate chip oatmeal cookies. Max had been begging his dad to make them for two weeks. Finally, his dad had a day off, and he told Max he would make the cookies. Wouldn't you know that today, of all days, the oven would not heat up!

Max just had to have some chocolate cookies. Max's dad tossed a cookbook to Max. He told Max to start looking through the cookbook to find something they could make without using the oven. Max smirked at the idea but thumbed through the cookbook anyway.

What do you know! Max found a chocolate oatmeal cookie recipe that did not need baking! The recipe was called "No-Bake Cookies." Max and his dad decided the recipe was worth a try.

Max and his dad read the recipe together. Then, his dad told Max to get out a saucepan. Max's dad got out the necessary ingredients, a big spoon, measuring cups and spoons, and some waxed paper.

Max's dad told him to put ½ cup milk, ¼ cup butter, 4 tablespoons cocoa, and 2 cups of sugar in a pan. They took turns stirring the mixture on the stove until it was bubbling on medium-high heat for one minute.

Once the hot mixture was pulled off the stove, Max's dad helped him add ½ cup peanut butter, 1 teaspoon of vanilla, and 2 cups of oatmeal. Max stirred. Then, Max dropped spoonfuls of the creamy mixture onto waxed paper. Max and his dad could not wait to try these interesting cookies once they had cooled!

The moment arrived. Max and his dad each bit into a "No-Bake Cookie." Delicious! Max was actually kind of glad the oven was broken! Now he and his dad had a new treat to make.

1 Number the events in order.

_____ Max got out the saucepan.

_____ Max learned that the oven was broken.

_____ Max and his dad took turns stirring the mixture.

_____ Max was ready to eat some of his dad's chocolate chip oatmeal cookies.

_____ Max and his dad enjoyed a delicious new treat.

_____ Max dropped spoonfuls of the chocolate mixture onto waxed paper.

_____ Max found a "No-Bake Cookie" recipe.

_____ Max thumbed through a cookbook.

2 How are no-bake cookies similar to cookies you bake? _____

_____

_____

3 Number the ingredients in the order in which they are needed.

_____ milk   _____ sugar   _____ oatmeal   _____ butter

_____ peanut butter   _____ cocoa   _____ vanilla

4 Why do you think Max dropped the cookies

onto waxed paper? _____

_____

_____

 On another sheet of paper, write the steps in order explaining how to brush your teeth.

An American Folk Hero

A **legend** is story that is set in the real world and includes some facts. The facts in a legend are often exaggerated.

John Henry was an African American railroad worker. He is a hero of many American legends in the South. The original story was created when the railroad was greatly expanding in the late 1800s. John Henry symbolized the workers' fight against being replaced by machines. A famous ballad, or song, tells how John Henry competed against a steam drill in a race to see whether a person or a machine could dig a railroad fastest. According to the legend, John Henry won the race, but died of exhaustion.

The Legend of John Henry

When John Henry was born, the earth shook and lightning struck. He weighed 44 pounds! Shortly after birth, baby John Henry reached for a hammer hanging on the wall. His father knew John Henry was going to be a steel-driving man.

Sure enough, John Henry grew up and worked for the railroad. He was the fastest, strongest steel-driving man in the world. No one could drive more spikes with a hammer than John Henry.

Around 1870, the steam drill was invented. It was said that this machine could dig a hole faster than 20 workers using hammers.

A company building a tunnel on one end of a railroad decided to try out the machine. John Henry's company was working on the other end of the tunnel, using men to drill. Both companies bragged and boasted that they were the fastest. Finally, the companies decided to have a race to see which was faster—the steam drill or man. It was John Henry against the steam drill.

Swinging a 20-pound hammer in each hand, John Henry hammered so hard that sparks flew! At the end of the day, he had beaten the drill by four feet! That night, John Henry lay down, very proud of his accomplishment, closed his eyes, and never woke up.

1 Number the events in order.

_____ John Henry hammered so hard that sparks flew.

_____ John Henry was born weighing 44 pounds.

_____ A company decided to try out the new steam drill.

_____ They decided to have a race to see if John Henry could beat the steam drill.

_____ John Henry beat the steam drill and then laid down and never woke up.

_____ Baby John Henry reached for a hammer hanging on a wall.

_____ John Henry grew up and became a steel-driving man.

2 Use context clues to find words from "An American Folk Hero" to match each definition. Then, write the letters in the matching numbered boxes below to learn an interesting fact about train tracks in the world.

growing   ___ ___ ___ ___ ___ ___ ___ ___
                      14   24   25   8

first or earliest   ___ ___ ___ ___ ___ ___ ___
                             5   11   10   13

stood for   ___ ___ ___ ___ ___ ___ ___ ___
                   4   27   26   17

achievement   ___ ___ ___ ___ ___ ___ ___ ___ ___ ___ ___ ___
                      12   9   22   7   2   21   18   1

boasted   ___ ___ ___ ___ ___ ___
           20   19   3

great fatigue   ___ ___ ___ ___ ___ ___ ___
              23   16   6   28   15

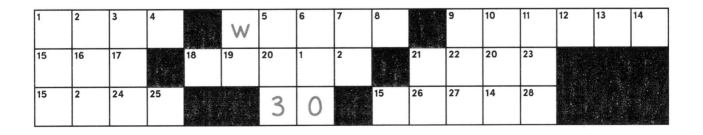

1	2	3	4			5	6	7	8		9	10	11	12	13	14
					W											
15	16	17		18	19	20	1	2		21	22	20	23			
15	2	24	25			3	0		15	26	27	14	28			

Too Much Talking

To better understand a story, careful readers **analyze,** or study, a character's personality, qualities, traits, relationships, motivations, and problems.

Logan is such a big talker. She drives Shauna and Maria crazy! Logan thinks she is great at everything. What makes Shauna and Maria even more frustrated with her is the fact that Logan IS good at everything. She always scores goals at soccer games. She scored the most points for the basketball team this year. She won first place overall in the city's swim competition. She always gets top grades on her spelling tests. She can finish a math test first and get the best score in the class. How can one person be so good at so much?

However, Logan is not good at one thing. She is not good at being a good sport. No matter what Logan does well, she makes sure everyone knows about it. She is also a little rude. Logan is quick to make comments about other kids' mistakes. If Shauna and Maria have to hear about one more goal they could have scored, or one more basket they should have made, or one more test they should have aced, they are going to scream! Shauna and Maria's one wish is that Logan learns to be humble.

Not many people tell Logan what a good job she does or congratulate her on her accomplishments because Logan has already boasted and bragged about them to everyone. She does not give anyone a chance to learn about anything she has done. She is always the first one to talk about her successes. Shauna and Maria sure wish Logan could be more like Aliyah.

Aliyah is the new kid in class this year. She does not talk much, but she is very good at many sports and is also super smart. It has taken the rest of the kids a while to learn about Aliyah and all her talents. Maria, Shauna, and the other kids are all happy to congratulate Aliyah when she scores a goal or gets a great score on a test. Aliyah just smiles and says thanks. She often makes a nice comment back to acknowledge someone's kindness, and she often compliments others at sporting events or on their schoolwork. Maria and Shauna have decided they want to learn to be more like Aliyah when they experience success. They wish Logan would learn from Aliyah, too. Unfortunately, she is always busy patting herself on the back.

1 Write words that describe Logan on her jersey. Write words that describe Aliyah on her jersey. Write words that describe both girls on the trophy.

> boastful   rude   thoughtful   insensitive   humble   intelligent   athletic   kind

2 List two examples of how Logan is not a good sport. _____

_____

_____

3 Why do many people usually not compliment Logan on her accomplishments?

_____

_____

4 Use context clues to find words from the story to match each definition.

not arrogant _____

impolite _____

remarks _____

annoyed _____

5 Whom do Shauna and Maria want to be like—Logan or Aliyah? Why?

_____

_____

Brian's Bike

Brian sat on his front doorstep. He really wanted a new bike. Marco had just gotten one for his birthday, and Dwayne's was only about a year old. Brian had owned his for five years. The seat was up as high as it could go, and his legs were still too long for his bike. Brian wanted a bike just like Marco's and Dwayne's. Their bikes were perfect for popping wheelies and cruising over bumps. If only he had $130. All he could come up with was $53. Where could he get the rest of the money he needed?

Brian thought and thought. His birthday was still five months away, and he was too young to mow lawns. What could he do to get the money? Maybe his dad would advance him his allowance for the next few months. He got $10 every Friday if he did all his chores. His dad had agreed to do this once before when Brian needed an extra $6. Maybe his sister would loan him the money. She had a lot of money saved up from baby-sitting. Baby-sitting! That was it! Brian could baby-sit. Oops! Wait a minute. No one would hire Brian to baby-sit. He still was not allowed to stay home by himself yet. What could he do to get the money? Brian sat and thought.

Just then, the phone rang. Mrs. Timmons' dog had gotten out again. She asked Brian if he could find Fifi for her. Brian said he would be happy to help Mrs. Timmons. She was getting so old. She could not run after feisty Fifi anymore. Brian immediately started looking for Fifi. He spotted her behind a tree in the Kirbys' yard.

After chasing Fifi through three different yards, Brian finally caught the frisky dog. He returned her to Mrs. Timmons. Mrs. Timmons was so thankful that she handed Brian $5. Brian thanked Mrs. Timmons and told her that she did not have to pay him. Then, Brian had an idea. Now he knew what he could do to earn money. He would set up a pet service! He could take care of people's pets when they were gone. He figured there were at least 12 dogs he could look after, a few cats, and even some fish. Brian would have that bike in no time!

1 Circle the words that describe Brian.

      lazy   optimistic   ungrateful   industrious

      whiny   stressed   hardworking   pessimistic

2 Why could Brian not baby-sit to earn money? _____

_____

3 If Brian's dad agreed to advance him his allowance, how many weeks of allowance

would Brian need to buy his bike? _____

4 If you were Brian's dad, would you advance his allowance for the bike?

Why or why not? _____

_____

_____

5 List Brian's ideas for getting the $77 he needs. Then, think of three additional ideas.

Brian's Ideas	Other Ideas
_____	_____
_____	_____
_____	_____

6 What should Brian do to get his pet service started? _____

_____

_____

7 How well do you think Brian will do with his new job? _____

_____

_____

Peaceful Protest

The United States has a long history of people working to make the country better for all. Peaceful **resistance** to unfair laws and practices has brought about positive changes.

Henry David Thoreau, born in Concord, Massachusetts, in 1816, has influenced the way many Americans **protest** unfair laws. Thoreau's essay "Civil Disobedience" urged people to use peaceful resistance to bring about changes in laws and government policies that they disagreed with. Thoreau's **principles** would **inspire** and influence future protesters in the United States and around the world. One example of this was during the American Civil Rights Movement.

Montgomery, Alabama, had a law separating bus passengers by race. African American passengers were required to sit in the back of the bus and to give up their seats to white passengers. On December 1, 1955, Rosa Parks, an African American woman, refused to give up her seat to a white man on a Montgomery bus. Parks was arrested. After her arrest, Dr. Martin Luther King, Jr., and a group of African American leaders organized a **boycott** of the Montgomery buses. It was a form of peaceful resistance to laws that **discriminated** against one group of people. For 381 days, African Americans walked or carpooled rather than use the buses. Dr. King was arrested. Threats were made against him and his family, but he and his followers held strong. They continued to boycott the buses and to hold peaceful marches to show their **opposition** to the unfair laws. In 1956, the United States Supreme Court declared Alabama's **segregation** laws unconstitutional. The protest was successful!

Dr. King's success inspired César Chávez, another believer in peaceful protest. In 1962, Chávez organized farm workers to protest low wages and poor working conditions. Chávez and members of the newly organized United Farm Workers of America (UFW) took a pledge to use only nonviolent methods to bring about change. Through organized protest marches, strikes, and a national boycott of grapes, Chávez and the UFW were able to improve the lives of **migrant** farmers. Farm workers earned higher pay and benefits and had safer working conditions. Although Chávez died in 1993, his work continues through the union he founded. In 1994, the Presidential Medal of Freedom, the highest civilian honor in the United States, was awarded **posthumously** to César Chávez.

1 Write four words that describe Rosa Parks and César Chávez.

_____ _____ _____ _____

2 Use the bold words from the article to complete the puzzle.

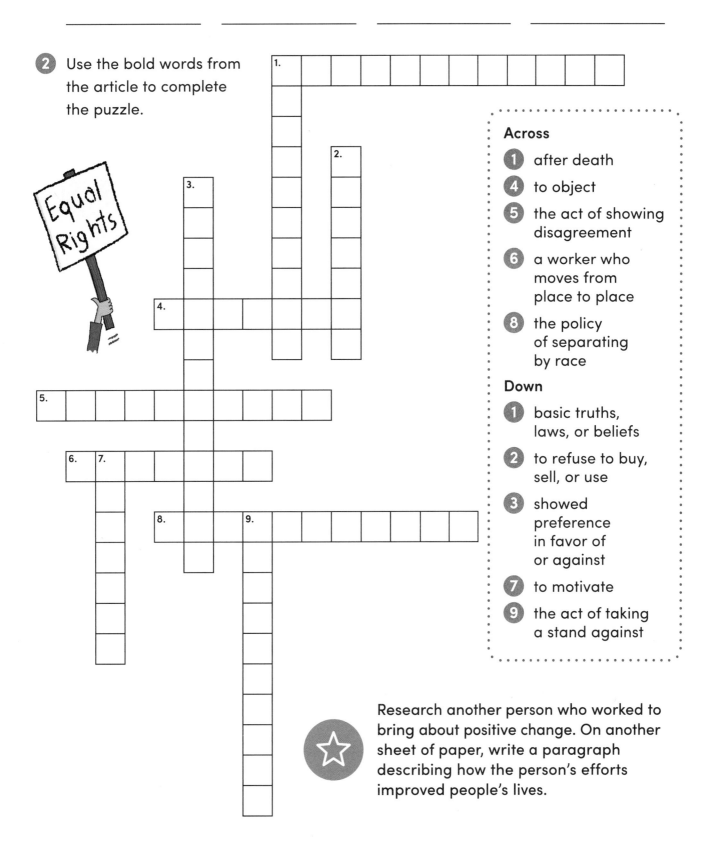

Across

1 after death

4 to object

5 the act of showing disagreement

6 a worker who moves from place to place

8 the policy of separating by race

Down

1 basic truths, laws, or beliefs

2 to refuse to buy, sell, or use

3 showed preference in favor of or against

7 to motivate

9 the act of taking a stand against

Research another person who worked to bring about positive change. On another sheet of paper, write a paragraph describing how the person's efforts improved people's lives.

Test Time

When you **make predictions** you use information from a story to predict what will happen next.

On Monday, Ms. Bunch announced to her class that there would be a test covering the 50 United States and their capitals on Friday. In addition to knowing each state's capital, students would have to fill in all the states' names on a U.S. map. Best friends Kevin and Matt both wanted to do well on the test, but each boy studied for the test in a very different way.

Kevin decided to wait until Thursday evening to begin studying. He thought if he learned everything on Thursday, he would be able to remember it better on Friday. After dinner Thursday evening, Kevin took his study notes into the family room so he could watch television while he studied. Ms. Bunch had given each student an alphabetical list of the states and their capitals. Kevin read the list over and over again. Then, he covered up the capitals and tried to remember what they were as he read each state's name. When he felt that he knew most of the capitals, he then took out his map and began studying where all the states were located. Since Kevin kept stopping to watch his favorite TV shows, he did not finish his studying until very late. The next morning, he skipped breakfast so he would not miss his bus.

Matt, on the other hand, took a different approach to his studying. On Monday evening, he made a set of flash cards. On one side of each card, he wrote the name of a state, and on the opposite side, he wrote the state's capital. He made one card for each state. He then traced the map of the United States, being careful to outline each state. He took this map to the copy store and made several copies. Now he had some maps to practice writing in the state names. After dinner on Tuesday, Wednesday, and Thursday, Matt spent an hour in his room studying his flash cards and practicing filling in his maps. His mom and dad also helped by quizzing him about the state capitals while he helped with cleaning up after dinner. On his way to school each day, Matt took his flash cards with him on the bus and practiced naming the capitals. Matt went to bed a little earlier on Thursday evening. The next morning, he had a good breakfast before catching his bus. On the way to school, he looked over his map and flash cards one last time.

When the boys arrived at school on Friday, they joined their classmates and prepared to take the big test. Matt and Kevin began to work hard to do their very best.

1. What mistakes do you think Kevin made in the way he studied? _____

_____

_____

_____

2. How was Matt's study plan different from Kevin's? _____

_____

_____

_____

3. Who do you think got a better score on the test, Kevin or Matt?

Explain your answer. _____

_____

_____

_____

On another sheet of paper, write about a test you thought you were prepared for, but it turned out you really were not. Read it to a friend.

A Storm Is Coming

A **cause** is what makes something happen. An **effect** is what happens as a result of a cause.

Olivia was so sad. She just couldn't believe it! She was supposed to have her birthday party tomorrow at Super Kool Skateboard Park, but now there was a chance that the city was going to get hit by a hurricane. The party would have to be rescheduled. At least Olivia's mom had already picked up her birthday cake, so now she could have two cakes.

The weather center had been keeping a very close eye on the hurricane. The fierce storm originated way out in the Atlantic Ocean near Africa. It was now quickly heading towards the southern part of the United States—somewhere near Miami, which is where Olivia lived. The storm had winds of up to 120 miles per hour. This made it a category three hurricane, and Olivia knew it could be very damaging. Her city had experienced several hurricanes. So instead of running around with her mom doing last-minute things for her party, Olivia was busy helping her mom update their hurricane safety kit. They needed new batteries for the flashlights and radios, fresh water, some canned goods, a new can opener, bread, peanut butter, and any other non-perishable food and drink items Olivia could talk her mom into buying. Their kit still had plenty of bandages, blankets, and diapers and baby food for her baby brother.

While Olivia and her mom were busy at the store, Olivia's dad was busy at the dock securing their boat. When he finished, he returned to the house and covered their windows with plywood that he had already cut for just this kind of emergency.

When all the preparations were done, Olivia's parents gathered their files of important papers, some cherished family photos, and a few clothes for everyone. They packed everything in their van.

Since Olivia's grandparents live in Atlanta, Olivia and her family will evacuate Miami and go stay with them for a few days. Hopefully, they will all be able to return soon. After all, sometimes winds cause hurricanes to change direction and miss their expected target completely. Olivia hopes this will happen, but she is also excited that she will get to visit her grandparents.

1 Write **C** for cause or **E** for effect for each pair of sentences.

_____ Olivia's birthday party had to be rescheduled.

_____ A hurricane was approaching Olivia's city.

_____ The hurricane was a dangerous category three.

_____ The weather center was watching the hurricane closely.

_____ Olivia's dad was prepared for the hurricane.

_____ Olivia's dad had plywood already cut for their windows.

2 Match each cause with its effect.

Cause

_____ Olivia's gets to visit her grandparents.

_____ Winds change their direction.

_____ The storm is very dangerous.

Effect

A. Sometimes hurricanes miss their expected target.

B. Olivia's family is evacuating.

C. Olivia is excited.

3 List the items Olivia's family have in their hurricane safety kit. _____

_____

_____

4 What other items might the family need? Why? _____

_____

_____

 On another sheet of paper, make a list of six items you would take with you if you had to evacuate for safety reasons. Write a reason why you selected each item.

A Super Space Place

The International Space Station (ISS) was built by thousands of people from 15 countries. All these people and countries want to find out if humans can one day live in space.

Floating 220 miles above Earth, the ISS is made up of many pieces that were put together by astronauts in space. The main part of the construction began in 1998. United States space shuttles and Russian rockets transported tools and pieces of the station to help finish building it. They assembled the pieces in space! It was completed in 2011.

It is the largest structure ever to float above Earth. Although the main construction is complete, the ISS will continue to evolve as astronauts go on new missions and conduct experiments.

Some of the questions that crews who built the space station and crews that continue to visit the station are trying to answer include: *How does space travel affect germs? Does the body break down food and nutrients differently in space?* Some day, the station may even serve as a launchpad for missions to other planets, such as Mars.

Because of its large size, the ISS needs a lot of power. This power comes from solar energy. To create solar energy, large panels are lined with special materials. These materials collect the sun's energy for power and change the sun's rays into electricity.

So what does it cost to build such a structure? It costs more than $150 billion. Although this may seem astronomical, it may be a small price to pay for a project that enables some of the world's finest scientists to work together, exploring space for the world's future.

1 Write *C* for cause or *E* for effect for each sentence.

_____ People want to know if humans can one day live in space.

_____ Fifteen countries built the International Space Station.

_____ The ISS is powered by solar energy.

_____ Panels are lined with special materials that change the sun's rays into electricity.

2 Write a word from the article to match each definition. Then, write each numbered letter on the matching blank below to find out the four most requested foods of astronauts.

constructed __ __ __ __ __
          14

very great __ __ __ __ __ __ __ __ __ __ __
          9   8   3   6

carried from one place to another

__ __ __ __ __ __ __ __ __
   2   5   13

substances needed for the life and growth of plants, animals, or people

__ __ __ __ __ __ __ __
12   11

having to do with the sun __ __ __ __ __
                          1   7

put together __ __ __ __ __ __ __ __ __
                            10   4

Four most requested foods

__ h __ __ __ __   __ __ __ k __ __ __ __
1   2   3 10 5   6   7 6   8   9 3   4

__ __ __ __ __ __ __ __
4 11 10 7 12 9 13 11

__ __ __ __ k
1   8 11 9

__ __ __ w __ __ __ __
14 2   7   12 3 11 1

3 How does the ISS crew spend its time?

_____

4 Why might $150 billion be a small price to pay for the ISS?

_____

_____

_____

Awesome Oceans

To make an inference is to figure out what is happening in a story from clues the author provides.

Zoe's class had been studying world geography for three weeks. She had never traveled very far. Someday, though, Zoe wanted to go surfing in the Pacific, the Atlantic, or the Indian ocean. The Arctic and the Southern oceans would be too cold for surfing.

To help the class learn about the world's oceans, Mr. Steele, the geography teacher, decided to make up a game. He divided the class into five teams, one for each ocean. Then, he assigned each team an ocean to research. After time for research, Mr. Steele asked one person from each team to write clues about the ocean they researched on the board. The other students would try to guess which ocean the clues described.

Elijah's team's ocean is the world's second largest ocean. It covers about 41,105,000 square miles. It borders many countries around the world including several countries in North America and South America to the west, and in Europe and Africa to the east.

Kaley's team's ocean is the smallest. It is about 6,100,000 square miles. This ocean is located at the top of the world. It borders Canada, the United States, Greenland, Norway, and Russia. Even in the summer, there are big floating ice pieces called floes.

Johnny listed his team's clues. Their ocean is the largest and deepest ocean in the world. It covers approximately 63,000,000 square miles. This ocean is so big that it makes up about one-third of Earth's surface! It borders many countries including the United States, Australia, Canada, Japan, and China.

Nathalie's team wrote clues for an ocean that is smaller than the Atlantic by about 13,265,000 square miles. Asia is to the north of this body of water, and Australia and Southeast Asia lie on the east.

Finally, it was Zoe's turn to list clues for her team. This ocean is larger than the smallest ocean by 14,227,000 square miles. It is located at the bottom of the world. The tallest and heaviest penguins in the world, the emperor penguin, call this ocean home.

After all the clues had been given, Mr. Steele gave each team a map. They were to write the name of each ocean based on the clues. Zoe's team figured out the answers right away.

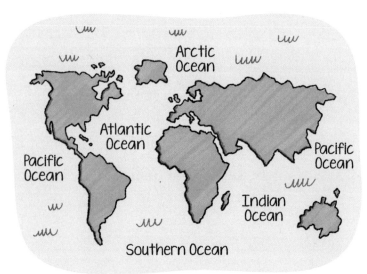

1 Complete the chart by writing each team's description in the correct column.

Team	Clues
Elijah	
Kaley	
Johnny	
Nathalie	
Zoe	

2 Use the clues to label the oceans on the map below.

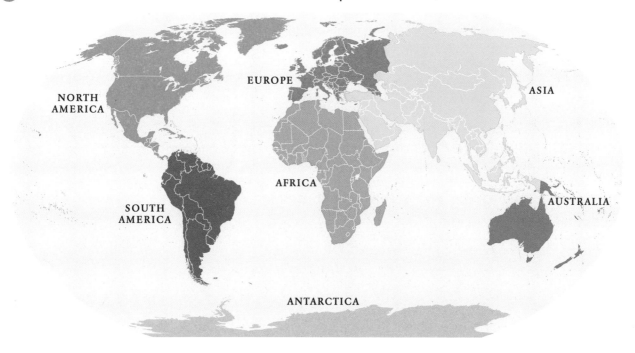

Green Gift

Poor Grandma! She had fallen and broken her leg. She would be in a cast for six weeks. Amy and Mark wanted to find a way to cheer her up.

"I have an idea," said Mark. "I saw a picture of a terrarium in a magazine. A terrarium is a little indoor garden that can be grown in a glass jar. Let's make one for Grandma."

Amy thought Mark had a great idea, so the two of them found the magazine article with the directions for making a terrarium and showed their mom. She agreed that it would be a perfect gift for Grandma. She helped Amy and Mark find a large, clear glass jar, which they cleaned and checked for leaks. After a trip to the garden shop to buy the materials, they were ready to assemble the terrarium.

First, they put a layer of charcoal and gravel at the bottom of the jar. This would keep the soil from getting too damp.

Draw a layer of charcoal and gravel at the bottom of the jar.

Next, they added a layer of dark, rich soil.

Draw a layer of dark soil on top of the drainage materials.

Now they were ready to add the plants. Mark used a long-handled spoon to tap out holes in the soil. Amy had chosen two plants at the garden shop. One was tall with long, thin, green leaves. The other was short with bright pink flowers. Mark placed the plants in the holes and gently tapped the soil down over their roots.

Draw the two plants Mark and Amy planted.

To make the terrarium even more colorful, Amy placed some colorful rocks and bright green moss around the plants.

Draw the colorful rocks and green moss that Amy added to the terrarium.

Finally, Mark and Amy lightly watered the plants in the terrarium. Now the terrarium was ready to take to Grandma.

When Amy and Mark showed Grandma her new terrarium, she was so happy. Now she had a beautiful little garden to enjoy right inside her home.

Mark and Amy want to make another terrarium for their Aunt Hilda's birthday, but they lost the magazine article with the directions. Help them make a new set of directions.

1 Make a list of all the materials Mark and Amy needed to assemble the terrarium.

_____   _____

_____   _____

_____   _____

_____   _____

_____   _____

2 What must be done to the jar before adding the materials to it? _____

_____

3 Tell how to assemble the terrarium. Be sure to use the steps in correct order.

First, _____

_____

Next, add _____

Now use a long-handled spoon to _____

    and then add _____

    and tap _____

To make the terrarium more colorful, place _____

_____

Finally, _____

_____

4 Why do you think Amy only chose two plants for the terrarium? _____

_____

_____

Sports Galore

To **classify** means to put things into categories with other similar things.

Carrie and Ryan were sitting under a tree, thinking about life. Carrie said, "You know, Ryan, I think I am going to be the next Serena Williams. She won 23 grand slam titles and was still playing tennis at 39! I can pound a pretty hard tennis ball over a net myself!"

Ryan was not very impressed. "If I wanted to, I could be the next Roger Federer. Roger holds the title for the most grand slam male singles titles with 20 titles so far. He's won eight Wimbledon titles, seven Australian Open titles, five U.S. Open titles, and one French Open title. However, I am saving my talents for the basketball court."

"The basketball court," laughed Carrie. "I am afraid you have a lot of growing to catch up with Michael Jordan! He's a superstar who is often called basketball's greatest all-time player. During his career, he averaged 30.1 points per game. He has also been named the NBA's MVP a total of five times!"

"Hey! I will get there—some day! My dad is over six feet tall. It will happen, and then you will be watching me slam dunk a basketball in a nice air-conditioned arena. No hot and humid or stormy weather for me. I like playing sports indoors."

"Well, that's fine," replied Carrie, "but you sure play a lot of football outside. I thought you might want to be the next Emmitt Smith. In 1995, Smith scored a record 25 touchdowns! It only took him seven seasons to score over 100 career touchdowns. This is the fastest accumulation of touchdowns in NFL history. You know, Ryan, you can toss the football pretty far."

"Carrie, I was thinking that since you love the cold, you might want to put on your ice skates and be the next Sarah Hughes. I can just see you getting excited when you win the gold medal for figure skating like she did in the 2002 Olympic Games."

"Well, thanks, Ryan," Carrie replied, "but I am not really much of a skater. Actually, I have always wanted to be an architect like my dad."

"Yeah, and I have always wanted to fly airplanes like my mom," said Ryan. The two grew quiet and just sat and thought—some more.

1 Write words from the story that fit each category.

Sports	Sports Equipment
_____	_____
_____	_____
_____	_____
_____	_____
_____	_____

2 Write the names of the famous athletes from the story on their matching sports items.

3 Who is your favorite sports figure? Why? _____

_____

_____

_____

_____

Read about other famous athletes. Add an athlete's name to each piece of sports equipment in question 2. On another sheet of paper, write one accomplishment each athlete achieved.

A Timely Business

To **draw conclusions** is to use the information in a story to make a logical assumption.

★ ★ ★ APRIL 14, 1860 ★ ★ ★

The mail did get through! The Pony Express mail delivery service is happy to announce that its riders finished the first complete run from Saint Joseph, Missouri, to Sacramento, California. It originated on April 3.

For those of you unfamiliar with the Pony Express, this impressive service employs men who ride fast ponies or horses, relay-style, across a 1,966-mile trail. These men carry letters and small packages. They promise delivery from one end of the trail to the other in 10 days or less!

Finally, there is a way to communicate long distance with friends and acquaintances. You will not have to rely on slow boats or stagecoaches. Over 80 riders, 400 fast horses, and 197 Pony Express stations make up the Pony Express. Its riders are generally of small build, and many are teenagers. A day's work consists of about a 75-mile trip, with stops at several stations. The stations are 5 to 20 miles apart. Riders earn about $100 to $150 a month.

The Pony Express operates both day and night to ensure timely delivery of important letters and packages. Its riders work in all kinds of weather. Be kind if you see a hard-working rider.

★ OCTOBER 26, 1861 ★

Sad news for the Pony Express. After operating for only about 19 months, the service closed its doors today. This came just 2 days after the opening of the transcontinental telegraph, a device that has revolutionized long-distance communication. Needless to say, the Pony Express faces huge monetary losses.

The closing comes just months after the Pony Express service boasted of a 7-day, 17-hour delivery from St. Joseph, Missouri, to Sacramento, California. The record-breaking ride delivered a copy of President Abraham Lincoln's first address to Congress.

1. What could have happened after the Pony Express closed? Select all that apply.

○ People stopped mailing letters.
○ Pony Express riders had to find new jobs.
○ There were many fast horses for sale.
○ More people started using the transcontinental telegraph.

2 What do you think would have happened to the Pony Express if it had stayed open after the transcontinental telegraph opened? Choose one.

○ The Pony Express would have hired more riders.

○ People would have stopped using the Pony Express once they realized how much more efficient the transcontinental telegraph was.

○ The Pony Express would have built several more trails for their riders to use.

3 How do you think people felt about the Pony Express closing? Explain your answer.

_____

_____

_____

4 Find words from the story to match each definition. Then, circle each word in the puzzle. The words go → and ↓.

hires and pays _____

brought about a major change _____

having a strong impact on _____

is made up of _____

people you know, but not very well _____

began _____

B	K	A	C	Q	U	A	I	N	T	A	N	C	E	S
R	E	V	O	L	U	T	I	O	N	I	Z	E	D	F
N	M	B	N	B	T	P	Y	E	O	R	P	L	G	T
T	P	A	S	I	S	K	P	W	K	V	P	E	R	A
K	L	N	I	M	P	R	E	S	S	I	V	E	Z	Y
X	O	L	S	T	S	F	V	N	V	K	Q	Y	V	D
U	Y	Q	T	A	E	T	X	U	X	Z	K	C	E	P
M	S	O	S	D	W	U	H	O	S	O	X	W	N	S
P	T	O	R	I	G	I	N	A	T	E	D	P	Q	L

From Pole to Pole

Antarctica and the Arctic region are the most southern and northern areas on Earth. These extremely cold areas have been the destinations for many scientific explorations.

Antarctica surrounds the South Pole. It is the coldest of the seven continents. Masses of ice and snow, about one mile thick, cover most of Antarctica's land. It is the most desolate place on Earth. Few plants can survive in its extreme cold, and its only wildlife lives on the coast.

There is no sunlight at all for months at a time in Antarctica. This keeps the continent very cold. In the winter, temperatures drop below -40°F on the coast and to about -100°F inland. Because it is so cold, little snow falls in this area. The South Pole only gets four to six inches of snow each year. However, the existing snow is packed so heavily and tightly that it has formed a great ice cap. This ice cap covers more than 95% of Antarctica.

It is probably not surprising that there are no cities or towns in Antarctica. In fact, no people live there permanently. Since Antarctica was discovered in 1820, many teams of scientists and explorers have braved its cold to learn about this interesting piece of land.

Although very little grows in Antarctica, the seacoast does have a variety of animal life. Whales, seals, penguins, petrels, and fish are among the animals that live in and near Antarctica's coastal waters. All of these animals depend on the sea for food and shelter.

On the opposite end of Earth is the North Pole. This is also a very cold region. It is called the Arctic. It includes the Arctic Ocean and thousands of islands. The northern parts of Europe, Asia, and North America are also part of this region.

Unlike Antarctica, the Arctic is a permanent home for many people. About 90 percent of all Arctic lands are free of snow and ice in the summer—except for Greenland. Although the sun never shines on much of the Arctic during the winter, it does shine on all parts of this area for at least a little while each day from March to September.

As in Antarctica, little plant life can survive in the Arctic. It is plagued not only by cold, but also by wind, a lack of water, and the long, dark winters. Willow trees do grow in the far north of the Arctic but are only a few inches high. A permanently frozen layer of soil, called *permafrost*, prevents roots from growing deep enough in the ground to properly anchor most plants. Therefore, even if plants can survive the cold, they do not grow roots deep enough to enable them to grow very large.

Because it is warmer than Antarctica, the Arctic is home to such animals as reindeer, caribou, bears, and sables. These animals live in pastures all over the Arctic. The seacoast is also home to many birds, including long-tailed ducks, eider ducks, falcons, geese, and loons.

1 Write *F* for fact or *O* for opinion.

_____ Antarctica is the coldest of all the continents.

_____ Farmers would be easily frustrated trying to get things to grow in the Arctic.

_____ There are no permanent residents in Antarctica.

_____ Antarctica is the most desolate place on Earth.

_____ The Arctic includes the northern parts of three continents.

_____ People who live in the Arctic enjoy Greenland about 90 percent of the time.

_____ Several kinds of animals live in the Arctic.

2 What is the main idea of the second paragraph?

○ Antarctica is the coldest place on Earth.
○ Antarctica is covered with huge amounts of ice and snow.
○ Antarctica is a very cold place and cannot support much life.

3 Underline the two sentences in paragraph eight that explain why few plants grow in the Arctic.

4 Why do you think people live in the Arctic but not in Antarctica? _____

_____

_____

5 Use context clues from the story to write a definition for each word below.

desolate _____

permanent _____

plagued _____

Loads of Fun

June 23

Dear Mom and Dad,

I am having a great time at camp. Yesterday, I went canoeing with my friends Tarik and Kayla. Boy, did we have a blast! Since it was so hot, we used our paddles to splash each other. We got a little carried away, but it was so much fun! Unfortunately, our counselor was not amused. The three of us had to mop the mess hall after dinner. I have become an expert mopper!

Would it be possible for me to stay at camp another two weeks? Just think, you would have another fourteen days of peace and quiet. This has been such an incredible learning experience. I am certain my school work next year will benefit from the additional camp time. I have already checked with the camp director. She said you just needed to call to verify that I can stay.

That's it for now. I hear Tarik calling me. Call the camp director as soon as you can.

Love,
Josh

Understanding an author's purpose can help you become a better reader. Authors write to **inform** (give readers facts), to **persuade** (convince readers to do or believe something), or to **entertain** (tell an interesting story).

1 What was Josh's purpose for writing the letter? _____

_____

_____

2 Do you think Josh's parents will let him stay at camp for two more weeks?

Why or why not? _____

_____

_____

 On another sheet of paper, change the above letter to show the other two types of an author's purpose.

ANSWER KEY

Page 5
1. The Washington Monument is a massive, impressive structure.
2. A visit to the Vietnam Veterans Memorial is a very moving experience.

Pages 6–7
1. The United States was threatened by French control of the Louisiana Territory.
2. While acquiring the Louisiana Territory greatly transformed the United States, Native American peoples were negatively impacted by the purchase.
3. Answers will vary.

Pages 8–9
1. She was looking for a real princess for the Prince to marry.
2. She had searched all over the world and had not found a real princess.
3. The real princess arrived at the palace during the terrible storm Tuesday night.
4. She hid a pea under 20 mattresses and 20 feather beds.
5. Answers will vary.
6. The authors feel it is a joyous occasion.
7. 1805, Denmark
8. They changed it to complete their writing assignment.

Pages 10–11
1. giant squid, octopus, shark, snail, sperm whale
2. They both have interesting eyes.
3. shark, sperm whale
4. albatross, caterpillar, giant squid, octopus, shark, snail, sperm whale
5. albatross
6. crocodile
7. They can move in two directions at the same time.
8. snail
9. sperm whale
10. giraffe

Pages 12–13
1. a. indulge b. pity
c. convenient d. famished
e. definitely f. nutritious
g. toxic h. distinctive
2.–4. Answers will vary.

Pages 14–15
1. a. partly b. established practice
c. over time d. bought
e. has the right to f. promised
g. basic h. faraway
i. area j. created
2. I, U
3. Alaska
4. Alaska and Hawaii
5. Answers will vary but should name three of the United States territories named in the article.

Pages 16–17
1. **Beethoven:** German, deaf, 1770-1827, *Moonlight Sonata*, piano, opera
Sousa: operettas, marches, American, *Semper Fidelis*, 1854-1932, United States Marine Band
Both: composer, influenced music, respected worldwide
2. Answers will vary.

Pages 18–19
1. **Ireland:** yes, yes, woman, blue shoe, marries prince
India: yes, yes, goat, nose ring, marries king
2. yes, yes, fairy godmother, glass slipper, marries prince
3. Cruel family members. The main character is beautiful and kind. There is a magic helper. There is an object that proves the main character's identity. There is a happy ending.
4. the type of magic helper and the object that proves the main character's identity
5. Answers will vary

Pages 20–21
1. 5, 2, 6, 1, 8, 7, 4, 3
2. Answers will vary.
3. milk = 1, sugar = 4, oatmeal = 7, butter = 2, peanut butter = 5, cocoa =3, vanilla = 6
4. Answers will vary.

Pages 22–23
1. 6, 1, 4, 5, 7, 2, 3
2. expanding, original, symbolized, accomplishment, bragged, exhaustion
They would circle the earth more than 30 times.

Pages 24–25
1. **Logan:** boastful, rude, insensitive
Both: intelligent, athletic
Aliyah: thoughtful, humble, kind
2. She boasts about her accomplishments. She makes comments about other kids' mistakes.
3. She has already boasted and bragged about them to other people. She does not give people a chance to congratulate her.
4. humble, rude, comments, frustrated
5. Shauna and Maria what to be like Aliyah because she is humble about her accomplishments and is kind to others.

Pages 26–27
1. optimistic, industrious, hardworking
2. He is too young to baby-sit.
3. 8 weeks
4. Answers will vary.
5. **Brian's Ideas:** have Dad advance allowance, borrow money from sister, begin a pet service
Other Ideas: Answers will vary.
6. Answers will vary.
7. Answers will vary.

Pages 28–29
1. Answers will vary.
2.

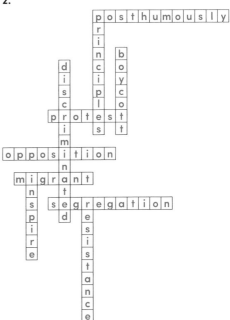

Pages 30–31

1. Possible answer: Kevin waited until Thursday to begin studying. He studied while watching television. He stayed up late studying. He skipped breakfast.

2. Matt began studying on Monday. He studied all week for the test. He made several types of review materials. He went to bed early the night before the test. He ate a good breakfast the morning of the test.

3. Answers will vary.

Pages 32–33

1. E, C; C, E; E, C

2. C, A, B

3. batteries, flashlights, radios, fresh water, canned goods, can opener, bread, peanut butter, non-perishable food and drink items, bandages, blankets, diapers

4. Answers will vary.

Pages 34–35

1. C, E; E, C

2. built, astronomical, transported, nutrients, solar, assembled

Four most requested foods by astronauts: **shrimp cocktail, lemonade, steak, brownies**

3. conducting experiments

4. Possible answer: because the ISS is a project that allows some of the world's finest scientists to work together, exploring space for the world's future

Pages 36–37

1. Elijah: second largest ocean, covers about 41,105,000 square miles, borders many countries including several in North America and South America to the west, and in Europe and Africa to the east

Kaley: smallest ocean, about 6,100,000 square miles, located at the top of the world, borders Canada, the United States, Greenland, Norway, and Russia, has ice floes even in summer

Johnny: largest and deepest ocean, covers approximately 63,000,000 square miles, makes up about one-third of Earth's surface, borders many countries including the United States, Australia, Canada, Japan, and China

Nathalie: smaller than the Atlantic by about 13,265,000 square miles, Asia is north of this body of water, and Australia and Southeast Asia lie to the east

Zoe: larger than the smallest ocean by 14,227,000 square miles, located at the bottom of the world, home to the emperor penguin

2.

Pages 38–39

1. large, clear glass jar, charcoal, gravel, dark soil, long-handled spoon, plants, colorful rocks, bright green moss, water

2. must be cleaned and checked for leaks

3. First, put a small layer of charcoal and gravel at the bottom of the jar. Next, add a layer of dark, rich soil. Now use a long-handled spoon to tap out holes in the soil and then add the plants and tap soil down over their roots. To make the terrarium colorful, place colorful rocks and bright green moss around the plants. Finally, water the plants.

4. Answers will vary.

Pages 40–41

1. Sports: tennis, basketball, football, figure skating

Sports Equipment: tennis ball, net, basketball, football, ice skates

2. tennis rackets: Serena Williams and Roger Federer, ice skate: Sarah Hughes, basketball: Michael Jordan, football: Emmitt Smith

3. Answers will vary.

Pages 42–43

1. Pony Express riders had to find new jobs., There were many fast horses for sale., More people started using the transcontinental telegraph.

2. People would have stopped using the Pony Express once they realized how much more efficient the transcontinental telegraph was.

3. Answers will vary.

4. employs, revolutionized, impressive, consists, acquaintances, originated

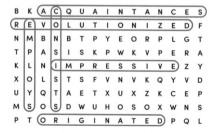

Pages 44–45

1. F, O, F, F, F, O, F

2. Antarctica is a very cold place and cannot support much life.

3. As in Antarctica, little plant life can survive in the Arctic. <u>It is plagued not only by cold, but also by wind, a lack of water, and the long, dark winters.</u> Willow trees do grow in the far north of the Arctic but are only a few inches high. <u>A permanently frozen layer of soil, called *permafrost*, prevents roots from growing deep enough in the ground to properly anchor most plants.</u> Therefore, even if plants can survive the cold, they do not grow roots deep enough to enable them to grow very large.

4. Answers will vary.

5. Answers will vary.

Page 46

1. to persuade

2. Answers will vary.